Remains Of Elmet
A Pennine Sequence

Poems by Ted Hughes

Photographs by Fay Godwin

Faber and Faber
London & Boston

Photographs printed by Fiona Hall

The book designed by Yvonne Skargon

First published in 1979
by Faber and Faber Limited
3 Queen Square London WC1N 3AU
Reprinted in 1981

Printed in Great Britain by
The Scolar Press, Ilkley

British Library Cataloguing in Publication Data
Hughes, Ted
Remains Of Elmet.
I. Title   II. Godwin, Fay
821'.9'14   PR6058.U37R/

ISBN 0-571-11395-8
ISBN 0-571-11426-1 Pbk

Remains Of Elmet

Poems in Memory of Edith Farrar

The photographs are for Ted

Six years into her posthumous life
My uncle raises my Mother's face
And says Yes he would love a cup of tea.

Her memory still intact, still good
Under his baldness.
Her hands a little plumper, trembling more
Chatter his cup in its saucer.

Keeping their last eighty years alive and attached to me,
Keeping their strange depths alive and attached to me.

He renews his prime exercising what happened,
As his body tries to renew its cells —

Air hijacked in the larynx
To fly a dream, populated with glimpses —

And the smoky valley opens, the womb that bore him,
Chimney above chimney, hill over hill,
A happy hell, the arguing immortal dead,
The hymns rising past farms —

He has brought me my last inheritance,
Archaeology of the mouth,
Treasures that crumble at the touch of day —

The huge fish, the prize of a lifetime,
Exhausted at the surface, the eye staring up at me,
But on such a frayed, fraying hair-fineness —

Any moment now, a last kick
And the dark river will fold it away.

The Calder valley, west of Halifax, was the last ditch of Elmet, the last British Celtic kingdom to fall to the Angles. For centuries it was considered a more or less uninhabitable wilderness, a notorious refuge for criminals, a hide-out for refugees. Then in the early 1800s it became the cradle for the Industrial Revolution in textiles, and the upper Calder became 'the hardest-worked river in England'.

Throughout my lifetime, since 1930, I have watched the mills of the region and their attendant chapels die. Within the last fifteen years the end has come. They are now virtually dead, and the population of the valley and the hillsides, so rooted for so long, is changing rapidly.

Fay Godwin set out to capture some impressions of this landscape at this moment, and her photographs moved me to write the accompanying poems.

TED HUGHES

Contents

Where The Mothers

Gallop their souls

Where the howlings of heaven
Pour down onto earth
Looking for bodies
Of birds, animals, people

A happiness starts up, secret and wild,
Like a lark-song just out of hearing
Hidden in the wind

A silent evil joy
Like a star-broken stone
Who knows nothing more can happen to it
In its cradle-grave.

Hardcastle Crags

"Think often of the silent valley, for the god lives there."
But here the leaf-loam silence
Is old siftings of sewing machines and shuttles,
And the silence of ant-warfare on pine-needles
Is like the silence of clogs over cobbles,
And the beech-tree solemnities
Muffle much cordite.

In a deep gorge under palaeolithic moorland
Meditation of conifers, a hide-out of elation,
Is a grave of echoes.
Name-lists off cenotaphs tangle here to mystify
The voice of the dilapidated river
And picnickers who paddle in the fringes of fear.
Far above, mown fields escape like wings.

But happiness is now broken water at the bottom of a precipice
Where the red squirrel drops shavings from a branch-end of survival
And beech-roots repair a population
Of fox and badger. And the air-stir releases
The love-murmurs of a generation of slaves
Whose bones melted in Asia Minor.

Lumb Chimneys

Days are chucked out at night.
The huge labour of leaf is simply thrown away.
Great yesterdays are left lying.

Nose upwind, the slogging world
Cannot look aside or backward.

Brave dreams and their mortgaged walls are let rot in the rain.
The dear flesh is finally too much.
Heirloom bones are dumped into wet holes.
And spirit does what it can to save itself alone.

Nothing really cares. But soil deepens.

And the nettle venoms into place
Like a cynical old woman in the food-queue.
The bramble grabs for the air
Like a baby burrowing into the breast.
And the sycamore, cut through at the neck,
Grows five or six heads, depraved with life.

Before these chimneys can flower again
They must fall into the only future, into earth.

15

These Grasses Of Light

Which think they are alone in the world

These stones of darkness
Which have a world to themselves

This water of light and darkness
Which hardly savours Creation

And this wind
Which has enough just to exist

Are not

A poor family huddled at a poor gleam

Or words in any phrase

Or wolf-beings in a hungry waiting

Or neighbours in a constellation

They are
The armour of bric-à-brac
To which your soul's caddis
Clings with all its courage.

Open To Huge Light

Wind-shepherds
Play the reeds of desolation.

Dragged out of the furnace
They rose and staggered some way.
It was God, they knew.

Now hills bear them through visions
From emptiness to brighter emptiness
With music and with silence.

Startled people look up
With sheeps' heads
Then go on eating.

Moors

Are a stage for the performance of heaven.
Any audience is incidental.

A chess-world of topheavy Kings and Queens
Circling in stilted majesty
Tremble the bog-cotton
Under the sweep of their robes.

Fools in sunny motley tumble across,
A laughter — fading in full view
To grass-tips tapping at stones.

The witch-brew boiling in the sky-vat
Spins electrical terrors
In the eyes of sheep.

Fleeing wraith-lovers twist and collapse
In death-pact languor
To bedew harebells
On the spoil-heaps of quarries.

Wounded champions lurch out of sunset
To gurgle their last gleams into pot-holes.

Shattered, bowed armies, huddling leaderless
Escape from a world
Where snipe work late.

The Trance Of Light

The upturned face of this land
The mad singing in the hills
The prophetic mouth of the rain

That fell asleep

Under migraine of headscarves and clatter
Of clog-irons and looms
And gutter-water and clog-irons
And clog-irons and biblical texts

Stretches awake, out of Revelations
And returns to itself.

Chapels, chimneys, vanish in the brightening

And the hills walk out on the hills
The rain talks to its gods
The light, opening younger, fresher wings
Holds this land up again like an offering

Heavy with the dream of a people.

It Is All

Happening to the sun.

The fallen sun
Is in the hands of water.

There are gulleys gouged in cold hills
By the sufferings of water

And gulleys
Cut in the cold fire

By the worn-out water of women
And the lost rivers of men.

Long Screams

Dark voices.
Swift weapons.

What rummaging of light
At the end of the world.

Unending bleeding.
Deaths left over.
The dead piled in cairns
Over the dead.
Everywhere dead things for monuments
Of the dead.

And now this whole scene, like a mother,
Lifts a cry
Right to the source of it all.

A solitary cry.

She has made a curlew.

Curlews in April

Hang their harps over the misty valleys

A wobbling water-call
A wet-footed god of the horizons

New moons sink into the heather
And full golden moons

Bulge over spent walls.

Curlews Lift

Out of the maternal watery blue lines

Stripped of all but their cry
Some twists of near-inedible sinew

They slough off
The robes of bilberry blue
The cloud-stained bogland

They veer up and eddy away over
The stone horns

They trail a long, dangling, falling aim
Across water

Lancing their voices
Through the skin of this light

Drinking the nameless and naked
Through trembling bills

Hill Walls

It set out —
Splendours burst against its brow
Broke over its shoulders.
The hills heeled, meeting the blast of space.

The stone rigging was strong.
Exhilarated men
Cupped hands and shouted to each other
And grew stronger riding the first winters.

The great adventure had begun —
Even the grass
Agreed and came with them,
And crops and cattle —

No survivors.
Here is the hulk, every rib shattered.

A few crazed sheep
Pulling its weeds
On a shore of cloud.

Walls

What callussed speech rubbed its edges
Soft and hard again and soft
Again fitting these syllables

To the long swell of land, in the long
Press of weather ? Eyes that closed
To gaze at grass-points and gritty chippings.

Spines that wore into a bowed
Enslavement, the small freedom of raising
Endless memorials to the labour

Buried in them. Faces
Lifted at the day's end
Like the palms of the hands

To cool in the slow fire of sleep.
A slow fire of wind
Has erased their bodies and names.

Their lives went into the enclosures
Like manure. Embraced these slopes
Like summer cloud-shadows. Left

This harvest of long cemeteries.

First, Mills

                          and steep wet cobbles
Then cenotaphs.

First, football pitches, crown greens
Then the bottomless wound of the railway station
That bled this valley to death.

A single, fatal wound. And the faces at windows
Whitened. Even the hair whitened.

Everything became very quiet.

The hills were commandeered
For gravemounds.

The towns and the villages were sacked.

Everything fell wetly to bits
In the memory
And along the sides of the streets.

Over this trench
A sky like an empty helmet
With a hole in it.

And now — two minutes silence
In the childhood of earth.

34

35

Hill-Stone Was Content

To be cut, to be carted
And fixed in its new place.

It let itself be conscripted
Into mills. And it stayed in position
Defending this slavery against all.

It forgot its wild roots
Its earth-song
In cement and the drum-song of looms.

And inside the mills mankind
With bodies that came and went
Stayed in position, fixed like the stones
Trembling in the song of the looms.

And they too became four-cornered, stony

In their long, darkening stand
Against the guerrilla patience
Of the soft hill-water.

Mill Ruins

One morning
The shuttle's spirit failed to come back
(Japan had trapped it
In a reconstructed loom
Cribbed from smiling fools in Todmorden).

Cloth rotted, in spite of the nursing.
Its great humming abbeys became tombs.

And the children
Of rock and water and a draughty absence
Of everything else
Roaming for leftovers

Smashed all that would smash
What would not smash they burned
What would not burn

They levered loose and toppled down hillsides.

Then trailed away homeward aimlessly
Like the earliest
Homeless Norsemen.

Wild Rock

        Tamed rock.
Millstone-grit — a soul-grinding sandstone.

Roof-of-the-world-ridge wind
And rain, and rain.

Heaven — the face of a quarry.
Oak-leaves of hammered copper, as in Cranach.
Grass greening on acid.

Wind. Cold. A permanent weight
To be braced under. And rain.

A people fixed
Staring at fleeces, blown like blown flames.

A people converting their stony ideas
To woollen weave, thick worsteds, dense fustians

Between their bones and the four trembling quarters.

The Sheep Went On Being Dead

Under the height's road, under crucified oaks
Among slovenly bracken
In the broken spine of a fallen land.

Happy work-hum of the valley mills
Stifled the shouting above looms
Which were too sunk in the pit anyway
To share the air-stir ironically
With the sheep's crumble of doll's curls and calcium.

It was a headache
To see earth such a fierce magnet
Of death. And how the sheep's baggage
Flattened and tried to scatter, getting flatter
Deepening into that power
And indrag of wet stony death.

Time sweetens
The melting corpses of farms
The hills' skulls peeled by the dragging climate —
The arthritic remains
Of what had been a single strength
Tumbled apart, forgetting each other —

The throb of the mills and the crying of lambs
Like shouting in Flanders
Muffled away
In white curls
And memorial knuckles

Under hikers' heels.

The Big Animal Of Rock

Is kneeling
In the cemetery of its ancestors.

In its home
Among its pious offspring
Of root and leaf.

In its homeland
Among a solemn kin
Who visit each other in heaven and earth.

Here

At the Festival of Unending
In the fleshly faith
Of the Mourning Mother
Who eats her children

The cantor
The rock,
Sings.

46

Tree

A priest from another land
Fulminated
Against heather, stones and wild water.

Excommunicated the clouds
Damned the wind
Cast the bog pools into outer darkness
Smote the horizons
With the jawbone of emptiness

Till he ran out of breath —

In that teetering moment
Of lungs empty
When only his eye-water protected him
He felt
Heaven and earth moving.

And words left him.
Mind left him. God left him.

Transfigured, bowed —
The lightning conductor
Of a maiming glimpse — the new prophet

Gasped a cry.

Heather

The upper millstone heaven
Grinds the heather's face hard and small.
Heather only toughens.

And out of a mica sterility
That nobody else wants
Thickens a nectar
Keen as adder venom.

A wind from the end of the sky
Buffs and curries the grizzly bear-dark pelt
Of long skylines
Browsing in innocence
Through their lasting purple aeons.

Heather is listening
Past hikers, gunshots, picnickers
For the star-drift
Of the returning ice.

No news here
But the crumbling outcrop voices
Of grouse.

A sea of bees, meanwhile, mapped by the sun.

49

Rock Has Not Learned

Valleys are not aware
Heather and bog-cotton fit themselves
Into their snugness, vision sealed

And faces of people that appear
Moist-eyed, confronting the whole work

With cries that wince out
Just as they shape and tear clear

The whispery husk bones of faces

Are ground into fineness of light
By a weight
And shadowy violence
Of blind skylines revolving dumbly

Ignorant in ignorant air

Remains Of Elmet

Death-struggle of the glacier
Enlarged the long gullet of Calder
Down which its corpse vanished.

Farms came, stony masticators
Of generations that ate each other
To nothing inside them.

The sunk mill-towns were cemeteries
Digesting utterly
All with whom they swelled.

Now, coil behind coil,
A wind-parched ache,
An absence, famished and staring,
Admits tourists

To pick among crumbling, loose molars
And empty sockets.

There Come Days To The Hills

Of Armadas about to set out —
Fresh mediaeval paintwork
Dragons on mainsails
A shouting throughout heaven

The moorlines cast off ropes, heaving their sides
Patched with harbour reflections
Turn into the light, nosing the distance
Strain in position, fluttering pennants

And the light itself leans taut
Tacking overtaking returning
Urgent and important

Everywhere exhilarated water

Even the sheep, standing windslapped
High in rigging
Look heroic

Every flashing face gazes Westward —

57

58

Churn-Milk Joan

A lonely stone
Afloat in the stone heavings of emptiness
Keeps telling her tale. Foxes killed her.

You take the coins out of the hollow in the top of it.
Put your own in. Foxes killed her here.
Why just here ? Why not five yards that way ?
A squared column, planted by careful labour.

Sun cannot ease it, though the moors grow warm.

Foxes killed her, and her milk spilled.

Or they did not. And it did not.

Farmers brought their milk this far, and cottagers
From the top of Luddenden valley left cash
In the stone's crown, probably in vinegar,
And the farmers left their change.

Churn-milk *jamb*. And Joan did not come trudging
Through the long swoon of moorland
With her sodden feet, her nipped face.
Neither snow nor foxes made her lie down
While they did whatever they wanted.

The negative of the skylines is blank.
Her legendary terror was not suffered.

Only a word wrenched, and the pain came,
And her mouth opened.

                          And now all of us,
Even this stone, have to be memorials
Of her futile stumbling and screams
And awful little death.

Grouse-Butts

Where all the lines embrace and lie down,
Roofless hovels of turf, tapped by harebells,
Weather humbler.

In a world bare of men
They are soothing as ruins
Where the stones roam again free.

But inside each one, under sods, nests
Of spent cartridge-cases
Are acrid with life.
Those dead-looking fumaroles are forts.

Monkish cells, communal, strung-out, solitary,
The front-line emplacements of a war nearly religious —
Dedicated to the worship
Of costly, beautiful guns.

A religion too arcane
For the grouse who grew up to trust their kingdom
And its practical landmarks.

I see a hill beyond a hill beyond a hill
Cries the hen-bird, with imperious eyes,
To her bottle-necked brood.

I see a day beyond a day beyond a day beyond a day
Cries the cock.

Too late, heads high and wings low
They curve in from heaven —
With a crash they pitch through stained glass
And drop on to a cold altar

Two hundred miles away.

High Sea-Light

Pearl-robe
Of earth's grit

Heaven glows through
Into the streams
Into gulping mouths

Into a world
Of busy dark atoms
Inside the live wreathed stone

Of light worn warm by a wonder.

The Weasels We Smoked Out Of The Bank

Ran along the rowan branch, a whole family,
Furious with ill-contained lightning
Over the ferny falls of clattering coolant.

After the time-long Creation
Of this hill-sculpture, this prone, horizon-long
Limb-jumble of near-female

The wild gentle god of everywhereness
Worships her, in a lark-rapture silence.

But the demons who did all the labouring
Run in and out of her holes

Crackling with redundant energy.

A Tree

Under unending interrogation by wind
Tortured by huge scaldings of light
Tried to confess all but could not
Bleed a word

Stripped to its root letter, cruciform
Contorted
Tried to tell all

Through crooking of elbows
Twitching of finger-ends.

Finally
Resigned
To be dumb.

Lets what happens to it happen.

Bridestones

Holy of holies — a hill-top chapel.
Actually a crown of outcrop rock —
Earth's heart-stuff laid bare.

Crowding congregation of skies.
Tense congregation of hills.
You do nothing casual here.

The wedding stones
Are electrified with whispers.

And marriage is nailed down
By this slender-necked, heavy-headed
Black exclamation mark
Of rock.

And you go
With the wreath of weather
The wreath of hills
The wreath of stars
Upon your shoulders.

And from now on,
The sun
Touches you
With the shadow of this finger.

From now on
The moon stares into your skull
From this perch.

Where The Millstone Of Sky

Grinds light and shadow so purple-fine

And has ground it so long

Grinding the skin off earth
Earth bleeds her raw true darkness

A land naked now as a wound
That the sun swabs and dabs

Where the miles of agony are numbness
And harebell and heather a euphoria

Spring-Dusk

                  — a frost-frail
Amethyst.

An iron earth sinking,
Frozen in its wounds.

A snipe
Knowing it has to move fast
Hurtles upwards and downwards

Drumming in the high dark — witchdoctor

Climbing and diving

Drawing the new
Needle of moon
Down

Gently

Into its eggs.

Football At Slack

Between plunging valleys, on a bareback of hill
Men in bunting colours
Bounced, and their blown ball bounced.

The blown ball jumped, and the merry-coloured men
Spouted like water to head it.
The ball blew away downwind —

The rubbery men bounced after it.
The ball jumped up and out and hung on the wind
Over a gulf of treetops.
Then they all shouted together, and the ball blew back.

Winds from fiery holes in heaven
Piled the hills darkening around them
To awe them. The glare light
Mixed its mad oils and threw glooms.
Then the rain lowered a steel press.

Hair plastered, they all just trod water
To puddle glitter. And their shouts bobbed up
Coming fine and thin, washed and happy

While the humped world sank foundering
And the valleys blued unthinkable
Under depth of Atlantic depression —

But the wingers leapt, they bicycled in air
And the goalie flew horizontal

And once again a golden holocaust
Lifted the cloud's edge, to watch them.

Sunstruck

The freedom of Saturday afternoons
Starched to cricket dazzle, nagged at a theorem —
Shaggy valley parapets
Pending like thunder, narrowing the spin-bowler's angle.

The click, disconnected, might have escaped —
A six! And the ball slammed flat!
And the bat in flinders! The heart soaring!
And everybody jumping up and running —

Fleeing after the ball, stampeding
Through the sudden hole in Saturday — but
Already clapped into hands and the trap-shout
The ball jerked back to the stumper on its elastic.

Everything collapsed that bit deeper
Towards Monday.

Misery of the brassy sycamores!
Misery of the swans and the hard ripple!

Then again Yes Yes a wild YES —
The bat flashed round the neck in a tight coil,
The stretched shout snatching for the North Sea —
But it fell far short, even of Midgeley.

And the legs running for dear life, twinkling white
In the cage of wickets
Were cornered again by the ball, pinned to the crease,
Chained to the green and white pavilion.

Cross-eyed, mid-stump, sun-descending headache!
Brains sewn into the ball's hide
Hammering at four corners of abstraction
And caught and flung back, and caught, and again caught

To be bounced on baked earth, to be clubbed
Toward the wage-mirage sparkle of mills
Toward Lord Savile's heather
Toward the veto of the poisonous Calder

Till the eyes, glad of anything, dropped
From the bails
Into the bottom of a teacup,
To sandwich crusts for the canal cygnets.

The bowler had flogged himself to a dishclout.
And the burned batsmen returned, with changed faces,
Like men returned from a far journey,
Under the long glare walls of evening

To the cool sheet and the black slot of home.

Willow-Herb

The canal sunning slack ripples,
Rusts, useless.

Black chimneys, lopped stump-low for safety,
Sprout willow-herb.

Down the Egyptian walls
The voices trickled

Into gleam-black stagnation.

Something that was fingers and
Slavery and religious, reflects sky.

Stone softens. Obsolete despair
Smiles this toothless and senile

Mauve-pink flower.

The Canal's Drowning Black

Bred wild leopards — among bleached depth fungus.
Loach. Torpid, ginger-bearded, secretive
Prehistory of the canal's masonry,
With little cupid mouths.

Five inches huge!
Over bridge reflections, I teetered
On the slime-brink, then a ringing, skull-jolt stamp
And their beards flowered sudden anemones

All down the sunken cliff. A mad-house thrill —
The stonework's tiny eyes
Two feet, three feet, four feet below me
Watched for my next move.

Their schooldays were over.
Peeping man was no part of their knowledge.
A Monkey god, a Martian
Tickled their underchins with his net rim

So they snaked out and over the net rim easy
Back into the oligocene —
Only restrained by a mesh of kitchen curtain
And flopped out of their ocean-shifting aeons

Into a two pound jam-jar
On a windowsill
Blackened with acid rain fall-out
From Manchester's rotten lung.

Next morning, Mount Zion's
Cowlèd, Satanic Majesty behind me
I lobbed — one by one — high through the air
The stiff, pouting, failed, paled new moons

Back into their Paradise and mine.

The Long Tunnel Ceiling

Of the main road canal bridge
Cradled black stalactite reflections.
That was the place for dark loach!

At the far end, the Moderna blanket factory
And the bushy mask of Hathershelf above it
Peered in through the cell-window.

Lorries from Rochdale, baled plump and towering
With worsteds and cottons, over my head met
Lorries from Bradford, and fought past each other
Making that cavern of air and water tremble —

Suddenly a crash!
The long gleam-ponderous watery echo shattered.

And at last it had started!
Bricks were dropping out of the tunnel ceiling,
The bridge was going to collapse!

But the canal swallowed its scare,
The heavy mirror reglassed itself,
The black arch gazed up at the black arch.

Till a brick
Rose through its eruption — hung massive
Then slammed back with a shock and a shattering.

An ingot!
Holy of holies! A treasure!
A trout
Nearly as long as my arm, solid
Molten pig of many a bronze loach!

There he lay — lazy — a free lord,
Ignoring me. Caressing, dismissing
The Eastward easing traffic of drift,
Master of the Pennine Pass!

Found in some thin glitter among mean sandstone,
High under ferns, high up near sour heather,

Brought down on a midnight cloudburst
In a shake-up of heaven and the hills
When the streams burst with zig-zags and explosions

A seed
Of the wild god now flowering for me
Such a tigerish, dark, breathing lily
Between the tyres, under the tortured axles.

Under The World's Wild Rims

Five hundred glass skylights, a double row,
Watched me, across the canal,
Halfway to school.

A thousand green skylights
Guarded a sacked tomb.

In submarine twilight, boots hushed
Ankle-deep through volcanic talc
Kicking up magical steel objects
For futuristic knobkerries.

Lifelines poured into wagepackets
Had leaked a warm horror, like Pompeii,
Into that worn-out, silent dust.

Vandal plumes of willow-herb
Desecrated the mounds —
Wild encampments, over crude fires
Converting the work-rich scrap to what they could eat.

Gradually five hundred skylights
Came within range. Five hundred stones
Gave my school-going purpose. One by one
Five hundred sunbeams fell on the horns of the flowers.

Two

Two stepped down from the morning star.
The stolen grouse were glowing like embers.
The dew split colour.
And a cupped hand brimmed with cockcrows.

Two came down with long shadows
Between the dawn's fingers
With the swinging bodies of hares
And snipe robbed of their jewels.

Then the stream spoke oracles of abundance
And the sun poured out at their feet.

Two dropped from the woods that hung in the sky
Bringing scorched talons of crows.
And the war opened —
                                    a sudden yelling
Ricochetted among close rooftops.

The guide flew up from the pathway.

The other stood still.

The feather fell from his head.
The drum stopped in his hand.
The song died in his mouth.

Mount Zion

Blackness
Was a building blocking the moon.
Its wall — my first world-direction —
Mount Zion's gravestone slab.

Above the kitchen window, that uplifted mass
Was a deadfall —
Darkening the sun of every day
Right to the eleventh hour.

Marched in under, gripped by elders
Like a jibbing calf
I knew what was coming.
The convicting holy eyes, the convulsed Moses mouthings.
They were terrified too.
A mesmerised commissariat,
They terrified me, but they terrified each other.
And Christ was only a naked bleeding worm
Who had given up the ghost.

Women bleak as Sunday rose-gardens
Or crumpling to puff-pastry, and cobwebbed with deaths.
Men in their prison-yard, at attention,
Exercising their cowed, shaven souls.
Lips stretching saliva, eyes fixed like the eyes
Of cockerels hung by the legs,
As the bottomless cry
Beat itself numb again against Wesley's foundation stone.

Alarm shouts at dusk!
A cricket had rigged up its music
In a crack of Mount Zion wall.
A cricket! The news awful, the shouts awful, at dusk —
Like the bear-alarm, at dusk, among smoky tents —
What was a cricket? How big is a cricket?

Long after I'd been smothered in bed
I heard them
Riving at the religious stonework
With screwdrivers and chisels.

82

83

The Ancient Briton Lay Under His Rock

Under the oaks, the polished leaves of Sunday.

He was happy no longer existing
Happy being nursery school history
A few vague words
A stump of local folk-lore.

A whorl in our ignorance.

That valley needed him, dead in his cave-mouth,
Bedded on bones of cave-bear, sabre-tooth.
We needed him. The Mighty Hunter.

We dug for him. We dug to be sure.

Stinging brows, Sunday after Sunday.
Iron levers.

We needed that waft from the cave
The dawn dew-chilling of emergence,
The hunting grounds untouched all around us.

Meanwhile his pig-headed rock existed.
A slab of time, it surely did exist.
Loyal to the day, it did not cease to exist.

As we dug it waddled and squirmed deeper.
As we dug, slowly, a good half ton,
It escaped us, taking its treasure down.

And lay beyond us, looking up at us

Labouring in the prison
Of our eyes, our sun, our Sunday bells.

85

Rhododendrons

Dripped a chill virulence
Into my nape —
Rubberised prison-wear of suppression!

Guarding and guarded by
The Council's black
Forbidding forbidden stones.

The policeman's protected leaf!

Detestable evergreen sterility!
Over dead acid gardens
Where blue widows, shrined in Sunday, shrank

To arthritic clockwork,
Yapped like terriers and shook sticks from doorways
Vast and black and proper as museums.

Cenotaphs and the moor-silence!
Rhododendrons and rain!
It is all one. It is over.

Evergloom of official tittivation —
Uniform at the reservoir, and the chapel,
And the graveyard park,

Ugly as a brass-band in India.

Crown Point Pensioners

Old faces, old roots.
Indigenous memories.
Flat caps, polished knobs
On favoured sticks.

Under the blue, widening morning and the high lark.

The map of their lives, like the chart of an old game,
Lies open below them.
Their yarning moves over it, this way and that,
Occupying the blanks.
Mills are missing. Chapels are missing.
But what has escaped the demolisher
Clings inside their masks —
Puppets of the graveyard's dreams.

Attuned to each other, like the strings of a harp,
They are making mesmerising music,
Each one bowed at his dried bony profile, as at a harp.
Singers of a lost kingdom.

Wild melody, wilful improvisations.
Stirred to hear still the authentic tones
The reverberations their fathers
Drew from these hill-liftings and hill-hollows
Furthered in the throats.

Moor-water toils in the valley.

An America-bound jet, on its chalky thread,
Dozes in the dusty burning dome.

Their vowels furl downwind, on air like silk.

For Billy Holt

The longships got this far. Then
Anchored in nose and chin.

Badlands where outcast and outlaw
Fortified the hill-knowle's long outlook.

A far, veiled gaze of quietly
Homicidal appraisal.

A poverty
That cut rock lumps for words.

Requisitioned rain, then more rain,
For walls and roof.

Enfolding arms of sour hills
For company.

Blood in the veins
For amusement.

A graveyard
For homeland.

Heptonstall

                              —old man
Of the hills, propped out for air
On his wet bench —
Lets his memories leak.

He no longer calls the time of day
Across to Stoodley, soured on that opposite ridge.
And Stoodley has turned his back
On the Museum silence.

He ignores Blackstone Edge —
A huddle of wet stones and damp smokes
Decrepit under sunsets.

He no longer asks
Whether Pecket under the East Wind
Is still living.

He raises no hand
Towards Hathershelf. He knows
The day has passed
For reunion with ancestors.

He knows
Midgley will never return.

The mantel clock ticks in the lonely parlour
On the heights road, where the face
Blue with arthritic stasis
And heart good for nothing now
Lies deep in the chair-back, angled
From the window-skylines,
Letting time moan its amnesia
Through the telegraph wires

As the fragments
Of the broken circle of the hills
Drift apart.

You Claw The Door

                              Rain
Crashes the black taut glass.

Lights in foundering valleys, in the gulf,
Splinter from their sockets.

Lights
Over conversation and telly and dishes
In graves full of eternal silence.

Lights
Of the wolf's wraith
That cannot any longer on all these hills
Find her pelt.

While the world rolls in rain
Like a stone inside surf.

Emily Bronte

The wind on Crow Hill was her darling.
His fierce, high tale in her ear was her secret.
But his kiss was fatal.

Through her dark Paradise ran
The stream she loved too well
That bit her breast.

The shaggy sodden king of that kingdom
Followed through the wall
And lay on her love-sick bed.

The curlew trod in her womb.

The stone swelled under her heart.

Her death is a baby-cry on the moor.

Haworth Parsonage

Infatuated stones.

Hills seeming to strain
And cry out
In labour.

Three weird sisters.

Imbecile silence
Of a stone god
Cut into gravestones.

The brother
Who tasted the cauldron of thunder
Electrocuted.

A house
Emptied and scarred black.

In a land
Emptied and scarred black.

Top Withens

Pioneer hope squared stones
And laid these roof slabs, and wore a way to them.

How young that world was!
The hills full of savage promise.

And the news kept coming
Of America's slow surrender — a wilderness
Blooming with cattle, and wheat, and oil, and cities.

The dream's fort held out —
Stones blackening with dogged purpose.
But at the dead end of a wrong direction.

And the skylines, howling, closed in —

Now it is all over.

The wind swings withered scalps of souls
In the trees that stood for men

And the swift glooms of purple
Are swabbing the human shape from the freed stones.

The Sluttiest Sheep In England

       that never
Get their back ends docked. Who
Doctors their wormy coughs ? Maggots
Bring them down in quarry dead ends
And the fluke reigns.

They get by
On the hill subsidy. Splash-black faces
Of psychotic mashams, possessed
By their demonic agates. They clatter
Over worthless moraines, tossing
Their ancient Briton draggle-tassel sheepskins
Or pose, in the rain-smoke, like warriors —

Eyes of the first water
Stare from perfunctory near-bald
Skulls of iguana
Like eyes trapped in helmets —

This lightning-broken huddle of summits
This god-of-what-nobody-wants
In his magnetic heaven
Has sent his angels to stare at you
In the likeness of beggars.

Auction

On a hillside, part farm, part stone rubble
Shitty bony cattle disconsolate
Rotten and shattered gear

Farmers resembling the gear, the animals
Resembling the strewn walls, the shabby slopes

Shivery Pakistanis
Wind pressing the whole scene towards ice

Thin black men wrapped in bits of Bradford
Waiting for a goat to come up

Widddop

Where there was nothing
Somebody put a frightened lake.

Where there was nothing
Stony shoulders
Broadened to support it.

A wind from between the stars
Swam down to sniff at the trembling.

Trees, holding hands, eyes closed,
Acted at world.

Some heath-grass crept close, in fear.

Nothing else
Except when a gull blows through

A rip in the fabric

Out of nothingness into nothingness

III

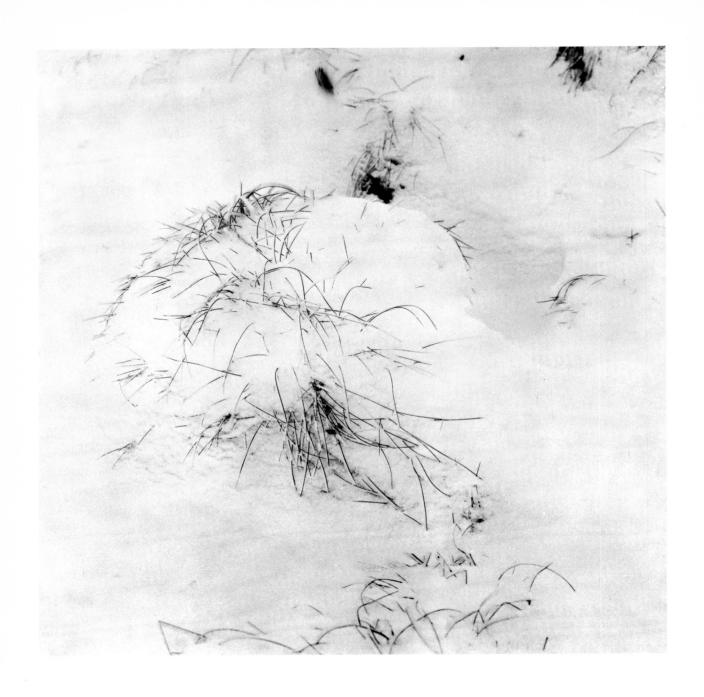

Light Falls Through Itself

Loses most of itself
And all its possessions.

Falls naked
Into poverty grass, poverty stone,
Poverty thin water.

Sees, sudden-close,
The smoking breath of a poor cow
Standing in thin mud.

Sees skylines blue far
Trembling like flames flattened under wind.

Wind without hindrance
Blows on the threadbare light
And through it.

Light creeps in grass
And cries
And shivers.

In April

The black stones
Bear blueish delicate milk,

A soft animal of peace
Has come a million years
With shoulders of pre-dawn
And shaggy belly

Has got up from under the glacier
And now lies openly sunning
Huge bones and space-weathered hide

Healing and sweetening
Stretched out full-length for miles —
With eyes half-closed, in a quiet cat-ecstasy.

116

The Word That Space Breathes

Through tumbled walls

Is accompanied
By lost jawbones of men
And lost fingerbones of women
In the chapel of cloud

And the walled, horizon-woven choir
Of old cares
Darkening back to heather

The huge music
Of sightlines
From every step of the slopes

The Messiah
Of opened rock.

Heptonstall Old Church

A great bird landed here.

Its song drew men out of rock,
Living men out of bog and heather.

Its song put a light in the valleys
And harness on the long moors.

Its song brought a crystal from space
And set it in men's heads.

Then the bird died.

Its giant bones
Blackened and became a mystery.

The crystal in men's heads
Blackened and fell to pieces.

The valleys went out.
The moorland broke loose.

Tick Tock Tick Tock

Peter Pan's days of pendulum
Cut at the valley groove.

Tick Tock Tick Tock
Everlasting play bled the whole unstoppable Calder
And incinerated itself happily
From a hundred mill chimneys.

Tick Tock Summer Summer
Summer Summer.
And the hills unalterable and the old women unalterable.
And the ageless boy
Among the pulsing wounds of Red Admirals.

Somebody else acted Peter Pan.
I swallowed an alarm clock
And over the school playground's macadam
Crawled from prehistory towards him
Tick Tock Tick Tock the crocodile.

Cock-Crows

I stood on a dark summit, among dark summits —
Tidal dawn splitting heaven from earth,
The oyster opening to taste gold.

And I heard the cockcrows kindling in the valley
Under the mist —
They were sleepy,
Bubbling deep in the valley cauldron.

Then one or two tossed clear, like soft rockets
And sank back again dimming.

Then soaring harder, brighter, higher
Tearing the mist,
Bubble-glistenings flung up and bursting to light
Brightening the undercloud,
The fire-crests of the cocks — the sickle shouts,
Challenge against challenge, answer to answer,
Hooking higher,
Clambering up the sky as they melted,
Hanging smouldering from the night's fringes.

Till the whole valley brimmed with cockcrows,
A magical soft mixture boiling over,
Spilling and sparkling into other valleys

Lobbed-up horse-shoes of glow-swollen metal
From sheds in back-gardens, hen-cotes, farms
Sinking back mistily

Till the last spark died, and embers paled

And the sun climbed into its wet sack
For the day's work

While the dark rims hardened
Over the smoke of towns, from holes in earth.

Heptonstall Cemetery

Wind slams across the tops.
The spray cuts upward.

You claw your way
Over a giant beating wing.

And Thomas and Walter and Edith
Are living feathers

Esther and Sylvia
Living feathers

Where all the horizons lift wings
A family of dark swans

And go beating low through storm-silver
Toward the Atlantic.

The Angel

In my dream I saw something disastrous.

The full moon had crashed on to Halifax.
Black Halifax boiled in phosphorus.
Halifax was an erupting crater.

The flames seemed to labour. Then a tolling glare
Heaved itself out and writhed upwards —
And it was a swan the size of a city!

Far too heavy for the air, it pounded towards me,
Low over Hathershelf.

And it was no swan.

It was an angel made of smoking snow.
Her long dress fluttered about her ankles,
Her bare feet just cleared the moor beneath her
Which glowed like the night-cloud over Sheffield.

Mother, I cried, O Mother, there is an angel —
Is it a blessing ? Then my mother's answer
Turned that beauty suddenly to terror.
I watched for the angel to fade and be impossible.

But the huge beauty would not fade.
She was cast in burning metal. Her halo
Was an enigmatic square of satin
Rippling its fringed edges like a flounder.

I could make no sense of that strange head-dress.

Till this immense omen, with wings rigid,
Sank out of my sight, behind Stoodley,
Under the moor, and left my darkness empty.